HAUS CURIOSITIES

Nonviolence

About the Author

RAMIN JAHANBEGLOO is an Iranian-Canadian philosopher. He is presently the executive director of the Mahatma Gandhi Centre for Nonviolence and Peace Studies and the vice-dean of the School of Law at O. P. Jindal Global University, Sonipat, India. He is the winner of the Peace Prize from the United Nations Association in Spain (2009) for his extensive academic work in promoting dialogue among cultures and his advocacy for nonviolence. More recently, he is the winner of the Josep Palau i Fabre International Essay Prize. Some of his most recent publications are *The Decline of Civilisation* (2017), *On Forgiveness and Revenge* (2017) and *The Global Gandhi: Essays in Comparative Political Philosophy* (2018).

Ramin Jahanbegloo

NONVIOLENCE

An Idea Whose Time Has Come

First published by Haus Publishing in 2023
4 Cinnamon Row
London SW11 3TW
www.hauspublishing.com

A CIP catalogue record for this book is
available from the British Library

Print ISBN: 978-1-913368-79-1
Ebook ISBN: 978-1-913368-80-7

Typeset in Garamond by MacGuru Ltd

Printed in Czechia

To my mother, whose unconditional love
has always been a lesson in nonviolence.

Contents

Nonviolence: An Idea Whose Time Has Come

'There is no greater power on earth than an idea whose time has come.'

Victor Hugo

The first time I came across the word 'nonviolence' was at the age of thirteen when I found a book about Mahatma Gandhi by Louis Fischer in my mother's private library.[1] In Iran, where I grew up, violence was always seen as a prerequisite for revolution and freedom. Iranian Marxists and Islamists considered revolutionary violence to be the natural solution for overthrowing the Shah's dictatorship. My parents, however, who never supported the Shah's regime, abhorred all forms of violence. Their strength of feeling was the first lesson in nonviolence that I received in my life. Yet despite this early introduction, I was not very familiar with the political aspects of nonviolence. It was only later, when I landed in Paris in

1974, that I heard some Latin American exiles describing their struggles against military dictators in Chile and Argentina as nonviolent. It didn't take me long to come across names such as Martin Luther King Jr, His Holiness the Fourteenth Dalai Lama, and Archbishop Desmond Tutu, and to start learning more about nonviolence and its history. Though fascinated by the moral courage of these political or spiritual characters, I was directly confronted and somehow distracted by all forms of violence, either from terrorist groups, such as the Baader-Meinhof Gang in Germany and the Red Brigades in Italy, or from revolutions, such as the Iranian and Nicaraguan revolutions of 1978–9. Moreover, nonviolence as a concept was never advocated by any of my classmates at Sorbonne University. As a matter of fact, among many politicised students at this time, violence was seen as a necessary evil for throwing off the yolk of oppression; some of them were even attracted to the anarchist ideas of Mikhail Bakunin and Peter Kropotkin. But the names of Mahatma Gandhi and Martin Luther King Jr were never mentioned in our philosophical and political discussions. Surprisingly, the concept of nonviolence was also absent in my collaborations with the French branch of Amnesty International (from 1977 to 1979) and other human rights groups in the 1980s. My enthusiasm for the Iranian revolution of

1979, combined with my academic works in the 1980s on thinkers such as Niccolò Machiavelli, Carl von Clausewitz, and Georg Wilhelm Friedrich Hegel, all of whom saw violence as a necessary evil in certain martial contexts, delayed the development of my early interest in the concept and reality of nonviolence.

It was in Paris in 1986, through a British classmate called John Smyth, that I came across the name of the American transcendentalist Henry David Thoreau and his famous essay 'On the Duty of Civil Disobedience', published in 1849. I was fascinated by his dissenting and anti-conformist tone and how he applied this to his abolitionist beliefs and writings. My readings of Thoreau and discussions with John took me back to my early encounters with the teachings of Mahatma Gandhi and Martin Luther King Jr, who were both deeply influenced by Thoreau's concept of civil disobedience. At the same time, I began collaborating with the journal *Esprit*, which was fundamentally sympathetic to the work of the French philosopher Paul Ricœur. My numerous personal encounters with Ricœur at the journal, followed by my reading of his famous essay of 1949 entitled 'Nonviolent Man and His Presence to History',[2] encouraged me to revisit the moral philosophy of Gandhi and to study his tremendous influence on the revival of the concept of nonviolence. My readings of Ricœur, and a close friendship with Olivier Mongin, Joël Roman, and Jean-Louis Schlegel, the management group of *Esprit*, changed the direction of my doctoral dissertation from Hegelian metaphysics to the intellectual origins of Mahatma Gandhi's concept of nonviolence. This was followed by a trip to India and a visit to Gandhi's Sabarmati Ashram in Ahmedabad, where I made the acquaintance of several of Gandhi's Hindu and Muslim collaborators who were still alive at the time.

What was so exceptional about *Esprit* was the number of intellectuals, writers, and civic actors who one could meet and exchange ideas with. In this way I got to know poets, writers, and civil society activists from Eastern Europe, who were actively engaged in their own nonviolent resistance against Communism in Eastern and Central Europe. Among these, I came to know a Czech poet in exile by the name of Jan Vladislav, who introduced me to the work of Václav Havel and invited me to the first meeting of the European Cultural Club (EKK) in January 1990 in Prague. A brief encounter with Havel helped me to understand the impact of Gandhian nonviolence in the long struggle of intellectuals, students, and artists against totalitarianism in Eastern and Central Europe. Havel's concept of 'the power of the powerless' (*Moc bezmocných* in Czech) had a huge impact on the evolution of Gandhian nonviolence in the second half of the twentieth century. The philosophy was further developed by the work of two other moral and political leaders, Nelson Mandela and the Dalai Lama, who applied Gandhi's teachings and their own native philosophies of Ubuntu and Tibetan Buddhism to their resistance of violence in South Africa and Tibet.

My first meeting with His Holiness the Fourteenth Dalai Lama was in April 2006. As a matter of fact, nonviolence and Mahatma Gandhi were the two subjects we talked about. At the time, I was living in India and working as a Rajni Kothari Chair in Democracy with the Centre for the Study of Developing Societies in Delhi. A few weeks later, on my return to Iran to meet with my mother, I was arrested at Tehran airport and held in solitary confinement for 125 days. I was accused of preparing a Velvet Revolution in Iran. Ironically, I have never been a member of a political group or party, but the simple fact of my writing on Mahatma Gandhi and the practice of nonviolence was enough to put me on the Iranian government's blacklist. I was finally released from prison and returned to India, and then moved with my family to Canada in 2008. Oddly enough, after my release from prison I was even more convinced that nonviolence is an idea whose time has come. For the past thirty years I have been teaching and writing about nonviolence. Today, I spend part of my time in India running the Mahatma

Gandhi Center for Peace Studies at O. P. Jindal Global University in Sonipat, Haryana, and the rest of the time I try to initiate students and civic actors around the world into nonviolence, its philosophical origins, its main figures, and its moral and political achievements.

This essay is about experiments and experiences with nonviolence that have been applied to different social justice struggles around the world. It aims to serve as a reminder of how individuals in history have confronted the question of violence. Unfortunately, in today's world we devote countless hours to learning about wars and violence but little to understanding nonviolence. Thinking and writing about nonviolence is not merely an academic exercise but an essential tool for the survival of human civilisation. For this reason, it is imperative that we investigate the idea of nonviolence and reflect upon it as a moral principle and philosophical ideal for creating a better future. In the past century, nonviolent resistance has been a strong spiritual and political method for overthrowing dictatorships and paving the transition to democracies around the world. Gandhi, King, Mandela, and Havel are only a few examples of leaders who have deployed nonviolence in their opposition to oppression, injustice, and hatred. Their message to each of us has been to champion moral courage, to stand up for what is right and just, and to work for a world of lasting peace and tolerance. Victor Hugo once remarked: 'There is no greater power on earth than an idea whose time has come.' Today, nonviolence is such an idea.

1

Gandhi and Nonviolence

We cannot speak about nonviolence without also understanding politics as the art of organising society, and the
means by which human beings construct a public realm.
We must also note that politics holds the potential for
collective freedom and justice, and as such is compat-
ible with nonviolence. Nonviolence, as an idea and as
a moral value, compels human beings to behave in a
specific manner predicated upon an interdependence
between ethics and politics. The uniting of politics and
ethics guarantees a possible exit from societal violence in
all its forms, while violent forms of political organisation,
such as tyranny and totalitarianism, inevitably lead to the
abandonment of ethics and reason in public life. In other
words, ethics start to leave the public space whenever and
wherever violence has been forced into the political.

In her controversial work *On Violence*, published in
1970, Hannah Arendt distinguishes clearly between the
two concepts of 'power' and 'violence'. As she says:

Power springs up whenever people get together and act in concert, but it derives its legitimacy from the initial getting together rather than from any action that then may follow. Legitimacy, when challenged, bases itself on an appeal to the past, while justification relates to an end that lies in the future. Violence can be justifiable, but it never will be legitimate. Its justification loses in plausibility the farther its intended end recedes into the future. No one questions the use of violence in self-defence, because the danger is not only clear but also present, and the end justifying the means is immediate.[3]

Although Arendt differentiates clearly between power and violence in her essay, she was not an unequivocal adherent of nonviolence. She believed that there are times in history when certain political struggles for freedom necessitate the use of violence. On this subject, she is clearly different from nonviolent leaders like Mahatma Gandhi, for whom violence was never justifiable or legitimate.

To properly understand the Gandhian idea of nonviolence, one needs to recognise the state of being nonviolent as the ability to act ethically in politics. Being nonviolent, in the ethical and political sense of the term, is a practice that only human beings, among all earthly creatures, seem to have developed in their history. Although the philosophy of nonviolence has been around for centuries in the form of religious teaching, Mahatma Gandhi was the first modern thinker and practitioner of nonviolence, who, true to the spirit of the ancient religions of India (Jainism, Buddhism, and Hinduism), translated the Sanskrit notion of *ahimsa* (non-injury) into the concept of nonviolence.

What inspired Gandhi go back to the particular notion of *ahimsa* and extend it into the domain of the political was his direct experience of colonial violence while growing up in India and later while living in South Africa, where he confronted the violent forces of militarism and imperialism. Precisely because Gandhi had experienced colonial violence in its most egregious form, he realised that the collapse of colonial oppression depends most of all upon the moral qualities and choices of those who are willing to confront it. Gandhi was especially critical of 'modern civilisation', as imposed on India by the British, which he saw as a mode of living that subordinated the quest for truth and spirituality in favour of pursuing power and money, and which he believed was responsible for many horrors of the modern world. As Gandhi put it, modern civilisation 'takes note neither of morality nor of religion. Its votaries calmly state that their business is not to teach religion ... This civilisation is irreligion.'[4] When Gandhi uses the words 'religion' and 'irreligion', he is not directing his followers towards institutionalised religion but rather to a code of ethics that syncretised the values of many different religions, and which were to be practised in both thoughts and deeds on one's path to self-realisation (which he interpreted as living in truth).

Gandhi saw nonviolence as the basic creed of human civilisation. He considered a civilised society to be a nonviolent society that was at peace with the world and free from fear and want. In this society there would be empathy and compassion among people, human beings would follow their duties and responsibilities, and self-centredness would be transformed into other-centredness, meaning moral attention to the Other rather than oneself.

Nonviolence was the goal of Gandhi's life and action. To reach that goal, he chose the path of truth. To him, truth, God, conscience, or the inner voice all meant the same thing. Gandhi's notion of nonviolence was based upon its reliance on the inner voice (the voice of conscience) as the bedrock of the soul-force (holding on to truth). Gandhi's belief in practising soul-force was fully developed in his method of *satyagraha* (a perpetual resistance against anything repugnant to the soul). As he wrote in his book *Hind Swaraj*:

Satyagraha is a method of securing rights by personal suffering; it is the reverse of resistance by arms. When I refuse to do a thing that is repugnant to my conscience, I use soul-force. For instance, the Government of the day has passed a law which is applicable to me. I do not like it. If by using violence I force the Government to repeal the law, I am employing what may be termed body-force. If I do not obey the law and accept the penalty for its breach, I use soul-force. It involves sacrifice of self.[5]

Gandhi's theory of nonviolence inseparably linked the political aim of self-rule in India with the moral duty of self-sacrifice. He saw the task of nonviolent action as compassionate and empathetic but also inclusive and educative, and applicable well beyond the political context of India. He believed that the philosophy of nonviolence was for all times and all places – a universal system promoting the values of tolerance, truthfulness, and trust, all of which were required for achieving Indian self-rule and human self-realisation more generally.

Gandhi argued, until the end of his life, that there was an essential relationship between means and ends, which he saw as exchangeable terms in his philosophy of nonviolence.

Nonviolence for me is not a mere experiment. It is part of my life and the whole of the creed of *satya-graha*, non-cooperation, civil disobedience, and the like, are necessary deductions from a fundamental proposition, that nonviolence is the law of life for human beings. For me it is both a means and an end.[6]

Gandhi was probably the first person in the history of political thought to forge a link between spiritual libera-tion and political nonviolence. This synthesis was based on what we can call a method of 'epistemic humility', which excluded the use of violence because of human beings' incapability of knowing the absolute truth. In this equation, the absence of arrogance goes hand in hand with recognising the absence of one's full knowledge of reality. From Gandhi's point of view, the individual's idea of truth was always contingent upon the perceptions of truth by others. Incidentally, Gandhi believed in a direct relationship between the two concepts of truth and love in the work of nonviolence. He affirmed: 'To see the uni-versal and all-pervading Spirit of Truth face to face one must be able to love the meanest of creation as oneself.'[7] As such, Gandhi made love the cornerstone of his non-violence. Indeed, one can find unmistakable traces of the teachings of Jesus in his Sermon on the Mount in *The Bhagavad Gita According to Gandhi*. Undoubtedly,

Mahatma Gandhi was a Hindu with a Christian heart. (This being said, only India could have produced a Mahatma Gandhi.) What attracted Gandhi to the Christian message of love was the nonviolent and compassionate character of Jesus himself. In Gandhi's view, Jesus of Nazareth, in the same way as Socrates, was a *satyagrahi* – a person who practises *satyagraha*, the pursuit of truth. As a pilgrim of truth, Gandhi drew wisdom from many different religions (including Islam, Buddhism, and Christianity) in order to give meaning and purpose to his nonviolent vision for the world. As such, Gandhi did not envision nonviolence as an ideology but as a spiritual state of mind, marked by moral courage and sympathy for the otherness of the Other. For Gandhi, nonviolence could not function as an instrument of change without being, at the same time, an effort to understand the Other in a spirit of dialogue and conviviality.

Gandhi's nonviolence was certainly marked with a great number of inconsistencies and imperfections, which he acknowledged himself. Gandhi never considered himself to be a person who was always philosophically and politically right. However, different historical and cultural attempts to engage with his philosophy of nonviolence in the past century have shown that Gandhi's life and thought represent a vivid and valid *modus operandi* for today's world. Thus, if Gandhi remains our contemporary, it is not just for his role in shaping the Indian nation but perhaps even more so for his theory and practice of nonviolence. Gandhi has been rightly sacralised by the Indian nation, but his positive influence, through his theory and action of nonviolence, has been universal. It is more important than ever that we take heed of his principle of nonviolence, to help change ourselves and the world.

2

Ethics and Politics: Loving Enemies

Mahatma Gandhi revolutionised the concept of nonviolence by framing it as both a moral and a political practice. His ethical revolution elevated the human value system and, as an expression of the ethically evolved self, the practice of nonviolence uplifted the individual.

Gandhian nonviolence was rooted in 'truth in action'. However, Gandhi spoke of truth in terms of personal experience rather than as a universal concept. Truth, for him, resided in every human heart, and one had to search for it there. This is how Gandhi established an essential relationship between his philosophy of nonviolence and common humanity. As a point of connection between ethics and politics, Gandhian nonviolence incorporated every religion, culture, and tradition of thought. He knew well that his philosophy transcended the specific circumstances and culture of India, and that it could be practised by members of all races, religions, and cultures. In a meeting on 21 February 1936 with an

African-American delegation sent to India by the US Student Christian Federation, Gandhi said: 'It may be through the Negroes that the unadulterated message of nonviolence will be delivered to the world.'[8] If one had to identify a start date for the US civil rights movement, the date of Gandhi's premonition may well be considered.

Mahatma Gandhi was not the only twentieth-century leader who preached nonviolence in their fight for truth and justice. Martin Luther King Jr drew significantly on Gandhian political philosophy and social strategy in his own struggle for African-American civil rights in the USA. What Dr King learned from Mahatma Gandhi was that no political act can be just and truthful unless it is morally legitimate. King was deeply influenced by his Christian upbringing, but his training years at Morehouse College followed by his graduate studies at Crozer Theological Seminary and Boston University also had a deep impact on his radical way of thinking, and in particular his belief in nonviolence: 'Not until I entered Crozer Theological Seminary in 1948 ... did I begin a serious intellectual quest for a method to eliminate social evil.'[9] After reading Nietzsche, Rousseau, Hegel, and Marx, King studied the teachings of Gandhi and observed:

> The intellectual and moral satisfaction that I failed to gain from the utilitarianism of Bentham and Mill,

the revolutionary methods of Marx and Lenin, the social contract theory of Hobbes, the 'back to nature' optimism of Rousseau, and the superman philosophy of Nietzsche, I found in the nonviolent resistance philosophy of Gandhi.[10]

Confronting the racial dilemma in the USA, King read Gandhian philosophy intensively as a new and powerful instrument against injustice. He recognised in Gandhi's philosophy of nonviolence an effective strategy for his own campaigns in areas such as integration and the voting rights of African-Americans. He became Gandhi's greatest disciple, embracing his *satyagraha* as a method of struggle for the emancipation of black people in America.

King arrived at his belief in nonviolence not only from reading Gandhi but also from his own metaphysical explorations of Christianity. As a Baptist minister, King drew extensively on the moral and theological foundations of the Christian faith. Central to his approach to spirituality was the idea of a knowable God. One has only to look at King's innumerable references to the idea of a 'personal God' and to 'the sacredness of human personality' to understand how personalism underscored his thoughts and civic actions as well as his approach to nonviolence. As he put it in his essay 'Pilgrimage to Nonviolence':

In recent months I have also become more and more convinced of the reality of a personal God. True, I have always believed in the personality of God. But in past years the idea of a personal God was little more than a metaphysical category which I found theologically and philosophically satisfying. Now it is a living reality that has been validated in the experiences of everyday life. Perhaps the suffering, frustration, and agonizing moments which I have had to undergo occasionally as a result of my involvement in a difficult struggle have drawn me closer to God. Whatever the cause, God has been profoundly real to me in recent months. In the midst of outer dangers I have felt an inner calm and known resources of strength that only God could give. In many instances I have felt the power of God transforming the fatigue of despair into the buoyancy of hope. I am convinced that the universe is under the control of a loving purpose and that in the struggle for righteousness man has cosmic companionship.[11]

King confronted the racial dilemma in the USA with anthropological optimism and with his solid belief that love would set the country on its path towards justice. He believed fundamentally that the arch of the moral universe bends towards justice and that a divine love operates in the human heart. Unsurprisingly, King's beliefs in the existence of God's justice and Christian love in the universe were essential to his efforts in applying the Gandhian strategy of nonviolence to the civil rights movement. Where Gandhi talked about soul-force, King insisted on the strength of love.

Love is the key concept of Martin Luther King Jr's philosophy of nonviolence. In King's view, in order to replace a segregated society in the USA with what he called a 'beloved community', Americans had to replace the love of power with the power of love. By describing the beloved community as a public sphere of interrelatedness and fellowship, King tried to draw an argument against the degrading and inhuman conditions of African-Americans in US society. He came to the conclusion that nonviolence is the only civic philosophy that can create a better social, political, and economic order.

To elucidate the kind of love he had in mind, King turned to three different Greek words for love: *Eros*, *Philia*, and *Agape*. He distinguished *Eros* as romantic love; *Philia* as friendly love; and *Agape* as a selfless love, an overflowing sentiment of empathy and compassion that seeks nothing in return. According to King, *Agape* love has a revolutionary power that one can find in the teachings of Jesus of Nazareth. King knew well that

African-Americans could only practise nonviolence as a mode of living through the exercising of *Agape* love. He realised that neither *Agape* nor his vision of the beloved community could be simply grounded on the philosophy of nonviolence as a political strategy. As he pointed out:

> It is quite possible, and even probable, that American Negroes will adopt nonviolence as a means, an instrument, for the achievement of specific and limited ends. This was certainly true in the case of Gandhi himself, for many who followed him, like Nehru himself, did so on this kind of basis. Certainly, it would be wrong, and even disastrous, to demand principled agreement on nonviolence as a precondition to nonviolent action. What is required is the spiritual determination of the people to be true to the principle as it works in this specific action. This was the case in Montgomery, and it will continue to be the rule in further developments of our struggle.[12]

King came to regard the Gandhian practice of nonviolence as a moment of loving enemies. He went to great lengths to make it clear that nonviolence was not a method for cowards but a way of demonstrating one's just cause by converting the opponent, without resorting to physical coercion. He wrote:

If you confront a man, who has long been cruelly misusing you, and say, 'Punish me, if you will, I do not deserve it, but I will accept it so that the world will know I am right and you are wrong,' then you wield a powerful and a just weapon. This man, your oppressor, is automatically morally defeated, and if he has any conscience, he is ashamed. Wherever this weapon is used in a manner that stirs a community's or a nation's anguished conscience, then the pressure of public opinion becomes an ally in your just cause.[13]

Martin Luther King Jr went to great lengths to make it clear to his fellow Americans and other people around the world that in a civic struggle for a just society we can never reach good ends through evil means. The philosophy of nonviolence teaches us that the nonviolent ends should pre-exist in the nonviolent means. Like Gandhi, King committed himself to a noble struggle for justice and equal rights. He refused to be a complacent and passive accomplice of a segregated and racist society, but he also never resorted to violent tactics or hypocrisy, both of which were all too evident in the Vietnam War and US foreign policy at the time.

When King was assassinated in April 1968, the USA lost its greatest moral leader. King was more than just the leader of the African-American civil rights movement.

He was an apostle of nonviolence who fought for the USA's conscience, in the same way that Mahatma Gandhi fought for India's soul. Two men, separated by time and continents yet connected by the practice of nonviolence. Ultimately, they both saw nonviolence as a way of life and an experiment in love. Dr King portrayed himself as 'a drum major of righteousness', a designation that can also be applied to Gandhi. As with Gandhi, King's belief in nonviolence hinged on a synthesis between ethics and politics. At the heart of this synthesis was the principle of love, which places compassion and mutuality at the centre of our lives.

And so we come full circle. The struggle to eliminate injustice and inequality goes hand in hand with the awakening of moral truth in one's opponents. What King teaches us in his writings and actions is that nonviolence is more than just an abstract philosophy or code of ethics to live by; it is also an indispensable method for resisting and overcoming the world's evils, and an essential political tool in humanity's struggle for a better world. Nonviolence as a philosophy matured through the words and actions of King, as evident from his prophetic piece entitled 'The Trumpet of Conscience', in which he asserted:

In a world facing the revolt of ragged and hungry masses of God's children; in a world torn between the tensions of East and West, white and colored, individuals and collectivists; in a world whose cultural and spiritual power lags so far behind her technological capabilities that we live each day on the verge of nuclear co-annihilation; in this world, nonviolence is no longer an option for intellectual analysis, it is an imperative for action.[14]

King's words, as well as Gandhi's, are lodestars in our contemporary social and political horizon, which continue to guide us on our path to nonviolence.

3

Civil Disobedience: Then and Now

'Massive civil disobedience', argued Martin Luther King Jr, 'is a strategy for social change which is at least as forceful as an ambulance with its siren on full.'[15] By saying this, he was pointing to the global potential of civil disobedience as a nonviolent mode of struggle. Both Mahatma Gandhi and Martin Luther King Jr came to discover the concept of civil disobedience through their readings of Henry David Thoreau. Thoreau published his famous essay 'Resistance to Civil Government', later known as 'On the Duty of Civil Disobedience', in 1849. About sixty years later, between October and December 1908, Mahatma Gandhi read Thoreau's essay during his second prison term in South Africa. He was deeply influenced by Thoreau's argument that every individual should follow higher laws and principles against all unjust laws.

As Anthony Parel summarised in his *Pax Gandhiana*:

Four ideas from this essay greatly impressed Gandhi. The first concerns the moral foundation of government and the state. To be strictly just, government must have the sanction of the governed. The second idea concerns the relationship of the individual to the state. In some respects, the individual is subject to the power of the state, but in some other respects, he or she is independent of it. Gandhi agreed with Thoreau that there would never be a truly free and enlightened state until the state recognised the individual as the higher and independent power from which all of its own power and authority are derived and treated him or her accordingly ... The third idea concerned the need to limit government's power over the citizen. 'That government is best which governs least' is the famous motto of Thoreau that Gandhi adopted as his own ... The fourth idea was that the duty to disobey an unjust law requires prompt, concrete action ... Thoreau's famous dictum that under a government that imprisons any person unjustly, 'the true place for a just man is also a prison', went straight to Gandhi's heart.[16]

Gandhi was impressed by Thoreau's moral courage and quest for truth, as well as his attachment to higher moral principles and his transcendentalist perception of reality.

In other words, Thoreau, like Gandhi, was a spiritual thinker, on a quest towards self-reform and the reforming of society. Interestingly, Thoreau never was a leader of the masses; he was considered by his contemporaries as a lonely man with an individualist character. His contribution to the history of nonviolence, therefore, came not through his actions but his words, in the form of his pioneering essay on civil disobedience.

Martin Luther King Jr was also strongly influenced by Thoreau's notion of dissenting disobedience, writing in *Stride Toward Freedom* about the Montgomery bus boycott of 1955–6:

> As I thought further I came to see that what we were really doing was withdrawing our cooperation from an evil system, rather than merely withdrawing our economic support from the bus company. The bus company, being an external expression of the system, would naturally suffer, but the basic aim was to refuse to cooperate with evil. At this point I began to think about Thoreau's essay 'Civil Disobedience'. I remembered how, as a college student, I had been moved when I first read this work. I became convinced that what we were preparing to do in Montgomery was related to what Thoreau had expressed. We were simply saying to the white

community, 'We can no longer lend our cooperation to an evil system.'[17]

Gandhi believed that the only way for individuals to defend their dignity and be in harmony with the moral essence of life was to disobey unjust laws. As for King, he quoted Saint Augustine on various occasions by repeating that 'an unjust law is no law at all'.[18]

These are just a few examples that demonstrate the significance of Thoreau's concept of civil disobedience in the nonviolent struggles of Mahatma Gandhi and Martin Luther King Jr. The keystone of Thoreau's essay and his doctrine of civil disobedience is our moral obligation to disobey. In a deeper sense, civil disobedience is a conscientious commitment to truth and a recognition of a moral framework in the universe. At the same time, it is a quest for self-examination.

Civil disobedience is the key nonviolent strategy left to us to fight for freedom and justice in society. It is a noble act of disloyalty that destroys our habit of obeying the state without asking questions. It also radically changes the definition of a law-abiding citizen. Thoreau argues in his essay that although democracy should be founded upon questioning, citizens tend to become servile and conformist, losing their will to dissent. He believed that the real task of nonviolent civil disobedience was to challenge and defeat the twin corruptions of democracy: imposed conformism and normalised complacency. Democracy has often been limited, or even destroyed, in recent history in the name of law and constitution. As Martin Luther King Jr observed in the early days of the civil disobedience movement he initiated in the USA: 'Democracy transformed from thin paper to thick action is the greatest form of government on Earth.'[19] And what is 'thick action' if not the nonviolent action of citizens in the public space? How can we talk about the democratisation of democracies if there is no 'publicness' of action and speech among its citizens? Nonviolence, therefore, is the citizen's capacity to act, to speak, and to create shared spaces through interaction with others. If there is one thing that the experience of nonviolent struggle in history shows us, it is that democratic govern-ance is not a power over a society but a power within it. In other words, if democracy equals self-rule and self-control of the citizens, empowerment of the civil society and the collective ability to rule democratically are the essential constituents of democratic governance. Democracy and nonviolence, therefore, are inseparable. Where democracy is practised, the rules of the political game should be defined by the absence of violence and a set of institutional guarantees against the domineering apparatus of the state.

In Thoreau's influential book *Walden*, which documents the two years he spent living simply in nature, he shows that freedom can only be attained in retreat from society. However, he believed equally in the reform of individuals through the reform of the society, as expressed in his essay 'On the Duty of Civil Disobedience'. Interestingly, Thoreau, as in the case of Gandhi and Dr King, did not see any unjust laws in nature. As Thoreau argued:

> Unjust laws exist: shall we be content to obey them, or shall we endeavour to amend them, and obey them until we have succeeded, or shall we transgress them at once? Men generally, under such a government as this, think they ought to wait until they have persuaded the majority to alter them. They think that, if they should resist, the remedy would be worse than the evil. But it is the fault of the government itself that the remedy is worse than the evil. It makes it worse.[20]

Thoreau's invitation to nonviolent disobedience is an act of democratisation that goes against Hobbesian philosophy, which argues that there is no social contract without the abandoning of one's natural rights, and therefore humans must surrender their will to a higher political power.

In the context of contemporary politics, two related questions come immediately to mind. First, if democracy is no more than a set of institutional guarantees, then citizens should be capable of thinking about politics beyond these institutions and struggling for the emergence of new perspectives of democratic action. Second, how are we to reconcile Thoreau's twin convictions that there can be no democracy unless the state's power is limited and that there can be no democracy without the pursuit of nonviolence? The answers to these two questions are related. On the one hand, humankind cannot escape politics without abdicating its humanity as a political animal. On the other, politics is not only the conquest and preservation of power. Politics, as described by the ancient Greek philosophers, should be the embodiment of ethics in a community. So not all politics is corrupt per se, and not all political powers are evil. However, polities that are conceived through violence will necessitate violent action to sustain their existence. That is to say, there is a paradox between the constitution of the political as an art of governing the society and the reality of violence. As a result, all attempts to contain the vital public space of citizens, as the exemplification of a shared community, marks the decline of a democracy. Henry David Thoreau was all too well aware of this when he invited his fellow

Americans to fight against slavery and the Mexican War by way of civil disobedience.

Civil disobedience was one of the central pillars identified in Gandhi's Constructive Programme – his treatise for gaining independence – alongside nonviolence, education, labour, hygiene, and economic equality. As he put it:

It is necessary to know the place of civil disobedience in a nationwide nonviolent effort.

It has three definite functions:

1. It can be effectively offered for the redress of a local wrong.
2. It can be offered without regard to effect, though aimed at a particular wrong or evil, by way of self-immolation in order to rouse local consciousness or conscience.
3. ...Civil disobedience can never be directed for a general cause such as for independence. The issue must be definite and capable of being clearly understood and within the power of the opponent to yield. This method properly applied must lead to the final goal ...

Civil disobedience is a stimulation for the fighters and a challenge to the opponent. It should be clear

to the reader that civil disobedience in terms of independence without the co-operation of the millions
by way of constructive effort is more bravado and
worse than useless.[21]

Mahatma Gandhi was very conscious of the limits of
civil disobedience as well as its potential to escalate. He
had experienced the mob fury of Chauri Chaura in February 1922, when the police opened fire on a large group
of protesters who retaliated by setting fire to a police
station, and he had decided to fast as a penance for
the violence of the demonstrators. Despite witnessing
these lapses into violence, civil disobedience remained a
central tenet in Gandhi's Constructive Programme and
campaign for social reform.

Gandhi was not the only moral leader who was confronted by mob violence while pursuing his nonviolent
strategy of civil disobedience. Martin Luther King Jr
experienced the same kind of chaotic and undisciplined
demonstrations in Memphis one week before his assassination on 4 April 1968. These violent demonstrators
were angry, young African-Americans, who preferred
separation to integration. Dr King was shattered by
this violence and vowed to continue with his policy of
civil disobedience. He knew well that nonviolence as a
concept and a mode of action was on trial. He declared:

Many people feel that nonviolence as a strategy for social change was cremated in the flames of the urban riots of the last two years. They tell us that Negroes have only now begun to find their true manhood in violence; that the riots prove not only that Negroes hate whites, but that, compulsively, they must destroy them ... If one can find a core of nonviolence toward persons, even during the riots when emotions were exploding, it means that nonviolence should not be written off for the future as a force in Negro life. Many people believe that the urban Negro is too angry and too sophisticated to be nonviolent ... I intended to show that nonviolence will be effective, but not until it has achieved the massive dimensions, the disciplined planning, and the intense commitment of a sustained, direct-action movement of civil disobedience on the national scale.[22]

While setting forth their visions for changing their societies and the world with the nonviolent strategy of civil disobedience, Gandhi and King did not ignore the need to address the practical obstacles to this method. They understood all too well the difficulties and limits of nonviolent action, and the psychological and cultural barriers that had to be overcome before civil disobedience could find full realisation.

Three decades after the assassination of Martin Luther King Jr, the events of the year 1989, when anti-communist revolutions swept across the Eastern Bloc, showed that nonviolence remained a potent method for social change. Today, the teachings and life experiences of Mahatma Gandhi and Martin Luther King Jr can help us in our nonviolent struggles against injustice, inequality, poverty, and discrimination around the world. They teach us that effective nonviolence can only be achieved through questioning and dissenting; that it necessitates an ethical voice and the individual right to be disloyal and resist unjust laws.

4

The Power of the Powerless:
Politics and Conscience

A nonviolent revolution is a revolution of values. As such, it is always in need of moral leaders. What history shows us is that the true actors of nonviolent change have always been politically powerless but morally powerful. By choice or by accident, this has been the role that people such as the Buddha, Jesus Christ, Socrates, Gandhi, King, Mandela, Havel, and the Dalai Lama have taken – people who gave up their pleasures and privileges to become peacemakers and moral guides of humanity.

At crucial moments in history, nonviolence tests the conscience of individuals and nations. It is the choice of life over death, of good against evil. It is a move past passivity, complacency, and conformism towards compassion, responsibility, and action. Politics in this framework is defined as the capacity to empathise with and understand the Other. This was the view of the late Czech president Václav Havel, another proponent of nonviolence and 'drum major' of the powerless, who emphasised the close relation between politics and conscience.

'It is becoming evident', wrote Havel, 'that truth and morality can provide a new starting point for politics and can, even today, have an undeniable political power.'[23] Although men of different times, Havel and Gandhi drew on similar principles in their quests for nonviolence and freedom. Instead of paying lip service to totalitarianism and supporting the communist regime, Havel ran the principle of moral responsibility past every political decision he made, with the goal of tapping into the power of the powerless. Havel is known to many around the world as a Czech dissident and later the president of the Czech Republic, but he was originally a poet and a playwright. He was one of the authors of the document Charter 77, which became a rallying point for opposition to communism in Eastern and Central Europe. Havel's political experiments in communist Czechoslovakia and the post-totalitarian state of the Czech Republic had a fundamentally ethical premise, which he called 'living in truth'. He saw the confrontation with absolute political power as a process of inviting powerless individuals to live in truth, justice, and decency. He argued:

When I speak of living within truth, I naturally do not have in mind only products of conceptual thought, such as a protest or a letter written by a group of intellectuals. It can be any means by which a person or a group revolts against manipulation: anything from a letter by intellectuals to a workers' strike, from a rock concert to a student demonstration, from refusing to vote in the farcical elections, to making an open speech at some official congress, or even a hunger strike, for instance. If the suppression of the aims of life is a complex process, and if it is based on the multifaceted manipulation of all expressions of life then, by the same token, every free expression of life indirectly threatens the post-totalitarian system politically, including forms of expression to which, in other social systems, no one would attribute any potential political significance, not to mention explosive power.[24]

Havel is focusing here on different modes of nonviolent resistance and dissent, which he considers to be different ways of living within truth. He advocates for the nonviolent path in confronting a totalitarian state, and invites the individual to regain a sense of responsibility and defend their dignity as well as their freedom. As such, Havelian nonviolent resistance followed in the tradition of Gandhian *satyagraha* in being a political and ethical means of holding onto truth. As well as being

an instrument of resistance that empowers the powerless against an unjust and tyrannical power, *satyagraha*
is also a moral tool that appeals to the conscience of the
individual. Havel expressed solidarity with and admira-
tion for fellow dissidents who chose an ethical course of
action even in the most immoral of environments and
let their conscience guide their political judgements.
According to Havel:

> The best resistance to totalitarianism is simply to
> drive it out of our own souls, our own circumstances,
> our own land, to drive it out of contemporary
> humankind ... A reaffirmed human responsibility
> is the most natural barrier to all irresponsibility ...
> I favour politics as practical morality, as service to
> the truth, as essentially human and humanly meas-
> ured care for our fellow humans. It is, I presume, an
> approach which, in this world, is extremely impracti-
> cal and difficult to apply in daily life. Still, I know no
> better alternative.[25]

When Havel speaks of politics as 'practical morality' and 'a service to truth', he is speaking directly to a
Gandhian tradition of nonviolence, in which politics
is equated with the ethical enterprise of self-realisation
in human beings. From Havel's point of view, political

action should always appeal to one's own conscience, and ethical principles should be the primary sources of nonviolent action. This is what he calls 'anti-political politics'. He affirms strongly:

> Yes, 'anti-political politics' is possible. Politics 'from below'. Politics of man, not of the apparatus. Politics growing from the heart, not from a thesis. It is not an accident that this hopeful experience has to be lived just here, on this grim battlement. Under the 'rule of everydayness' we have to descend to the very bottom of a well before we can see the stars.[26]

As a believer in nonviolence, Havel saw the real political struggle as the end of capture of power. As with Gandhi and King, by focusing on concepts such as conscience and belief, Havel argued for the importance of a spiritual dimension in the realm of politics. Perhaps the best example of this appears in his *Summer Meditations*, where Havel affirms: 'Acting sensitively in a situation does not exclude morality, but is more likely to accompany it, be bound to it, and even derive from it, because it comes from the same source – responsible thinking, attentiveness, and a dialogue with one's own conscience.'[27] The strong element of spirituality in Havel's nonviolent ethics is also evident in his essay 'Politics,

Morality, and Civility', in which he insists upon the 'spiritualisation of politics': 'I am convinced that we will never build a democratic state based on rule of law if we do not at the same time build a state that is – regardless of how unscientific this may sound to the ears of a political scientist – humane, moral, intellectual and spiritual, and cultural.'[28]

Havel's leadership is a great example of nonviolent thinking being applied to institutional politics. He was committed to the practice of nonviolence all his life, even if he was not fully Gandhian in deed and action. He was very conscious of the fact that nonviolence cannot be achieved with one's head in the sand. Havel believed that nonviolent democratic theory can be practised only when we can look at it clearly and critically.

It was in the spirit of dissidents such as Václav Havel that the Berlin Wall began to crumble. As the spirit of 1989 rose in East Berlin and began to spread throughout Eastern and Central Europe, the Poles, Czechs, Slovaks, Romanians, Hungarians, Lithuanians, Estonians, and Ukrainians came to understand that the empowerment of the powerless and the collective ability to rule democratically were the essential constituents of a nonviolent transition to democracy. But they were also reminded of the fragility of the human condition and the frailty of the public and political realms. Ironically, on the same day

(4 June 1989) that the communists were overwhelmingly defeated in Poland, leading to the peaceful fall of communism in that country, the Chinese pro-democracy movement was crushed by tanks in Tiananmen Square, but the lesson of nonviolence remained intact and more relevant than ever. The massacre of the Chinese students in Tiananmen Square was not the first time in history that an authoritarian regime has responded to strategic nonviolent action with coercion and violence. On this occasion, humanity realised once again not only that violence destroys the dream of a better future but also that nonviolence is not always victorious against evil. Nonviolent movements may not always triumph over hate and violence, but they are always worth pursuing.

Living With Nonviolence:
The Gandhian Moment

The Gandhian moment that took shape in the year 1989, also known as the Fall of Communism, when pro-democratic revolutions swept across Eastern Europe, reminded us that nonviolence is a viable *modus operandi* for effecting social and political change. This spirit of anthropological optimism and ethical politics resurfaced once again in the young Tunisians who shook Arab history through their use of nonviolent tactics in the Arab Spring of 2010–11.

In the decade since, nonviolent movements have sprung up in Algeria, Iran, Hong Kong, Myanmar, and many other countries globally. These movements show that the Gandhian spirit that inspired the Fall of Communism in 1989 and the students in Tiananmen Square is well and truly alive.

Despite their geographic and cultural diversity, nonviolent movements around the world have all been inspired by Gandhi's strategy for checking power and opposing violence through political transparency, reconciliation, and mutual respect. India's struggle for independence and the African-American civil rights movement showed that, far from being a utopian philosophy, nonviolence is one of our most practical means of resisting oppression – one which, when successful, leads to peaceful and democratic outcomes. This has been reflected in many nonviolent resistances since, such as the Polish Solidarity and Czechoslovakian Velvet Revolution of 1989, South Africa's struggle against Apartheid, and the Tunisian Jasmine Revolution of 2011.

Almost all revolutions in human history have been vengeful and bloody, and too often the resulting regimes have been unforgiving and resentful. Mahatma Gandhi was one of the first revolutionaries in history to draw on the positive power of nonviolence. His struggle was a political success, resulting in not only the peaceful termination of eighty-nine years of British colonial rule but also the creation of the world's largest democracy, which became a reality on 15 August 1947 and continues to this day. The subversive sweetness and radical tenderness of Gandhi's philosophy of nonviolence represented a fork in the road of human history.

For Gandhi, and later King, the greatest challenge of nonviolence was to remain ethical in the most unethical of environments, but the potential rewards for doing so were immeasurable. Within this framework, Gandhi rejected the notion that the ends should ever justify the means; for him, the two were one and the same: 'They say "means are after all means". I would say "means are after all everything". As the means so the end.'[29]

As a practice, nonviolence describes a move in the direction of empathy, compassion, and maturity, but it is also the transfer of speech, action, and power from politicians, oligarchs, and plutocrats to ordinary citizens. As such, it is an expression of true democracy and the *sine qua non* of any democracy that wishes to be built upon the principles of truth and love rather than lies and retribution. It is a philosophy that preserves our civilisation from self-destruction.

More than that, nonviolence is an expression of the freedom and autonomy of the individual. In the 1780s, the German philosopher Immanuel Kant described the Enlightenment as a movement that released human beings from 'self-incurred tutelage'.[30] It was the means by which humanity could become free of intellectual guardianship and learn to 'dare to think' (*Sapere aude*). Kant believed that this tutelage occurred because of many reasons, including cowardice and complacency. For Kant, being free meant being able to think and act independently of others. This intellectual maturity is where the force of nonviolent action resides; it helps people pursue not only their own political autonomy but also their intellectual and moral independence. Where there is a desire and impulse among the citizens of a society to think for themselves, to resist conformity and 'self-incurred tutelage', there are also strong foundations for nonviolence.

Gandhi, King, Mandela, and many others have shown that the truly civilised party in a clash for maturity, autonomy, and independence is the one that practises nonviolence. This has been the moral imperative and the intellectual foundation of all moral, spiritual, and political struggles in the history of humankind.

Freedom is never gained without truth-seeking. Even when truth is repressed, it will always rise again. After all, nonviolence cannot function without the moral courage to stand up and fight for justice. Nonviolence is rarely achieved without sacrifice and love for the Other. As Martin Luther King Jr put it: 'Love is the only force capable of transforming an enemy into a friend.'[31] Similarly, Nelson Mandela had the audacity to seek reconciliation with his opponents. Because of the absence of revenge and retaliation in his fight for freedom, Mandela was a leader with moral capital, which was further accumulated through his empathetic ethics and his respect for the otherness of the Other. This behaviour was in part influenced by his upbringing within the African philosophy of Ubuntu, which described a quality of empathy and compassion. In this way he resembled a nonviolent *satyagrahi* in the tradition of Gandhi. It was in this spirit that Mandela chose to join hands with his enemies, affirming: 'All South Africans must now unite and join hands and say we are one country, one nation, one people, marching together into the future.'[32]

Though Mandela's Ubuntu-esque approach didn't always win comprehensive approval in South Africa, it succeeded in dragging the country out of years of hatred and bloodshed. As he declared in a lecture in Oxford in July 1997: 'The spirit of Ubuntu – that profound African sense that we are human only through the humanity of other beings – is not a parochial phenomenon, but has added globally to our common search for a better world.'[33]

It is often taken for granted that great people can only attain the status of legends by using violence or extreme force. But figures such as Gandhi, King, Mandela, Mother Teresa, and Khān Abdul Ghaffār Khān are more than legends; they are moral leaders of human history. They taught us that when our hearts are filled with hate and anger, we cannot think straight, and they guided us to walk softly and moderately towards a better future for our children. If we agree that all life is interconnected, we must also conclude that nonviolence is the only true way forward. Therefore, the most important task of the philosophy of nonviolence today is to develop our habit of questioning and exploring new modes of living together.

Our age is one of strong views and political passions – often magnified through the medium of social media – which often translate into partisan hatred and aggression. The attitude and philosophy of nonviolence, with its underlying emphasis on loving one's enemy, has the potential to bridge these divides, to foster peaceful debate and enlightened ideas.

For the time being, however, the world is suffering from compassion fatigue and a lack of faith in our shared humanity. A reawakening of the philosophy of nonviolence is therefore essential if we want to work towards harmony among nations and cultures. We should not allow any individuals or peoples to pull humanity so low as to compromise its self-respect and noble spirit. Nonviolence is today the most important tool for the empowerment and enlightenment of humanity. As long as humanity remains in the grip of mediocrity and violence, nonviolence will be our leading light. Whether we like it or not, the Gandhian moment possesses the key to our salvation. We ignore it at the risk of our own future.

Notes

1. Louis Fischer, *The Life of Mahatma Gandhi* (London, 2006).
2. Paul Ricœur, 'Nonviolent Man and his Presence in History' in *History and Truth* (Evanston, 2006).
3. Hannah Arendt, *On Violence* (New York, 1970), 52.
4. Mahatma Gandhi, *Hind Swaraj and Other Writings*, ed. Anthony J. Parel (Cambridge, 1997), 37.
5. Ibid, 90.
6. Mahatma Gandhi, *The Essential Writings* (Oxford, 2008), 58.
7. K. Kripalani, *All Men Are Brothers: Life and Thoughts of Mahatma Gandhi as Told in His Own Words* (Ahmedabad, 1960).
8. Peter Eisenstadt, 'When Gandhi Introduced America's Civil Rights Leaders to Nonviolence', *Daily Beast* (2021).
9. Martin Luther King Jr, 'Pilgrimage to Nonviolence' in *Stride Toward Freedom: The Montgomery Story* (Boston, 2010), 78.
10. Ibid, 85.

11. Martin Luther King Jr, *A Testament of Hope: The Essential Writings and Speeches of Martin Luther King Jr*, ed. James Melvin Washington (New York, 1991), 40.

12. Martin Luther King Jr, 'The Negro is Part of That Huge Community Who Seek New Freedom in Every Area of Life' (1959).

13. King Jr, *A Testament of Hope*, 348.

14. Martin Luther King Jr, *'In a Single Garment of Destiny': A Global Vision of Justice* (Boston, 2012), 132.

15. Ibid, 125.

16. Anthony J. Parel, *Pax Gandhiana: The Political Philosophy of Mahatma Gandhi* (Oxford, 2016), 191–3.

17. King Jr, *Stride Toward Freedom*, 39.

18. King Jr, *A Testament of Hope*, 293.

19. Clayborne Carson, ed., *The Autobiography of Martin Luther King Jr* (New York, 2001), 60.

20. Henry David Thoreau, 'On the Duty of Civil Disobedience' in *Walden and Civil Disobedience* (Massachusetts, 1965), 241.

21. Gandhi, *Hind Swaraj and Other Writings*, 179–80.

22. King Jr, *'In a Single Garment of Destiny'*, 126–9.

23. Václav Havel, 'Politics and Conscience' in *Open Letters* (London, 1991), 270.

24. Ibid, 150–1.
25. Ibid, 269.
26. Ibid, 271.
27. Václav Havel, *Summer Meditations* (New York, 1993), 100–1.
28. Ibid, 18.
29. Gandhi, *All Men Are Brothers*, 134.
30. Immanuel Kant, 'What Is Enlightenment?' in *On History*, ed. Lewis White Beck (Indianapolis, 1963), 3.
31. Martin Luther King Jr, *The Words of Martin Luther King Jr* (New York, 1987), 4.
32. Peter Haine, *Mandela: His Essential Life* (London, 2018), 149.
33. Nelson Mandela, 'From Freedom to the Future' in *In His Own Words*, eds. Kader Asmal, Wilmot James, and David Chidester (London, 2003), 324.